# Animals in Our World

Poems and Photos by

## Judith Ryan

Judith Ryan has published her writing and photography in Northwest newspapers and magazines for the past 40 years. She's had a studio, doing portraits, weddings and events, as well as nature fine art prints. Last year Judith wrote and published her first book, "Mastectomy Moments". Combining writing and photography gives her great satisfaction. Using these skills to amuse her grandchildren provides her the most joy. Hence, this collection of poems and photos about animals, which she hopes will entertain children of all ages ~ yes, grownup children too!

**Animals In Our World** is available at Amazon and Create Space eStore

https://www.createspace.com/4961283
https://www.amazon.com/dp/1500906727
https://www.amazon.co.uk/dp/1500906727
**Judith@JudithRyanAuthor.com**

ISBN-13: 978-1500906726
ISBN-10: 1500906727
Publisher: Judith Ryan
Printed by: Create Space

Cover Photo by Judith Ryan
Interior Photos & Text by Judith Ryan
Book Interior designed by Judith Ryan
Author's photo by William B. Gould

# Dedication

This book is dedicated to my three grandchildren ~ William, Eleanor and Gianna. I love sharing these stories and pictures of animals with them. Through their sense of wonder, mine is renewed.

With Love,
Grandma Judith

# Table of Contents

# Animals in Our World ~ Introduction

This book of poems and pictures is a celebration of the variety of animals that live in our world. I feature animals I've met and photographed in different places and situations. Each encounter was a little adventure that made my life richer.

On the beach in Hawaii, I found the giant sea turtle. At a nature reserve in Canada I met the grey wolf and a big brown bear. Closer to home at the Seattle zoo, I had the opportunity to see many wondrous animals from around the world, especially Africa where the lions, zebras, elephants, giraffes and gorillas are found. And that's also where a gorgeous peacock strutted through the courtyard, raising and spreading his fantastically colorful feathers ~ like he was putting on a show.

A big surprise occurred at Golden Gardens, a waterfront park in Seattle. I was photographing the waves when a baby seal appeared in the surf just before it was tossed on the beach and landed at my feet! The city's Green Lake Park is full of interesting creatures to watch in their natural habitat. Ducks, turtles, squirrels, geese, herons and birds live there, while lots of dogs visit the lake to walk their owners.

When I think about all the different shapes, colors and behaviors of animals, I really have to smile. I hope reading about and seeing these pictures will bring a smile to your face too.

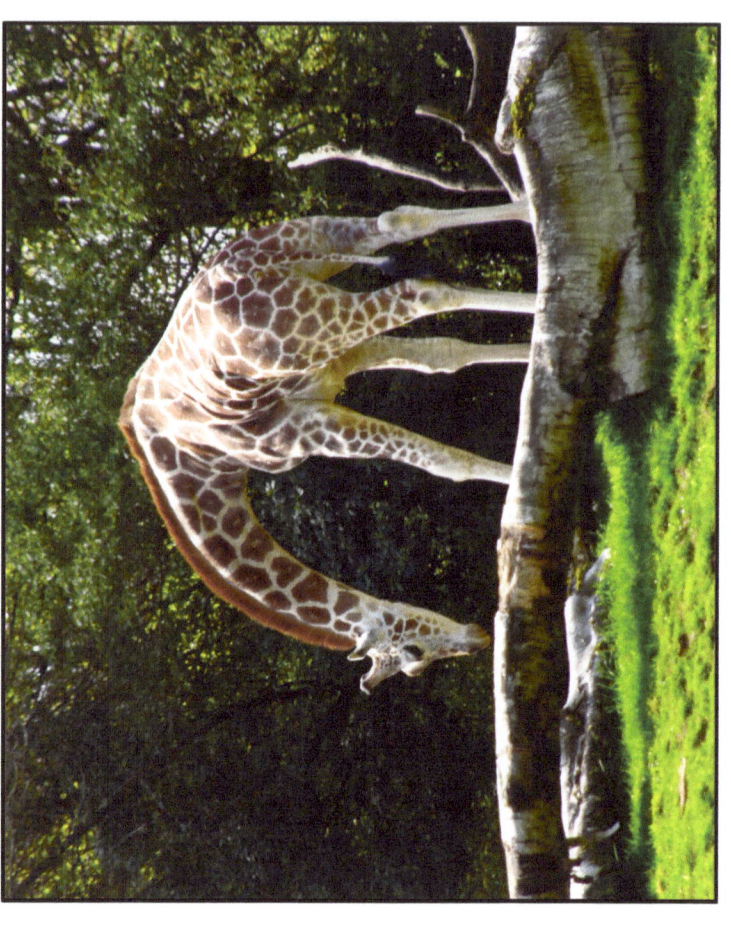

# Giraffe ~ an Unlikely Animal

Quite tall, with a veeery long neck ~
an animal from Africa, that's a giraffe.
They look so unlikely, but I try not to laugh.

With graceful movements,
their skinny legs carry about
a smallish head with a pointed snout.

The giraffe's brown patterned coat
is also quite worthy of note.
It's no wonder I enjoy their uniqueness.

And here's a good thing ...
when the food supply below stops,
they can still eat leaves off the treetops.

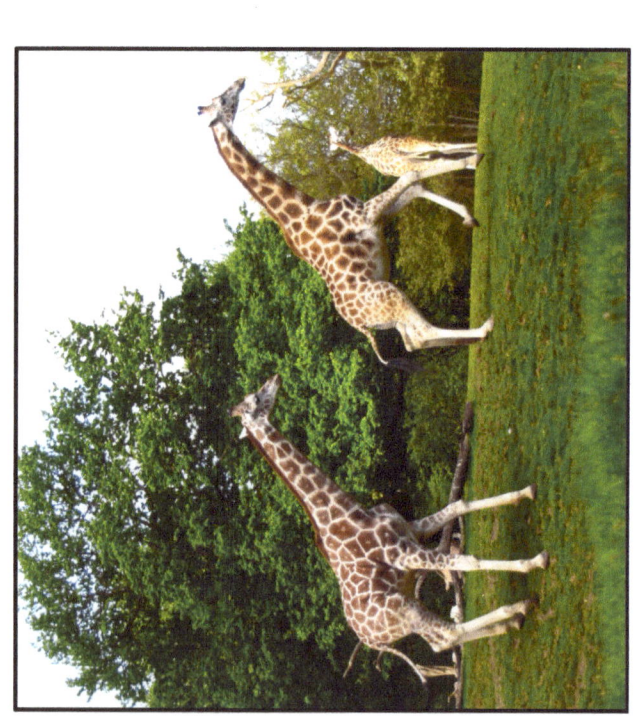

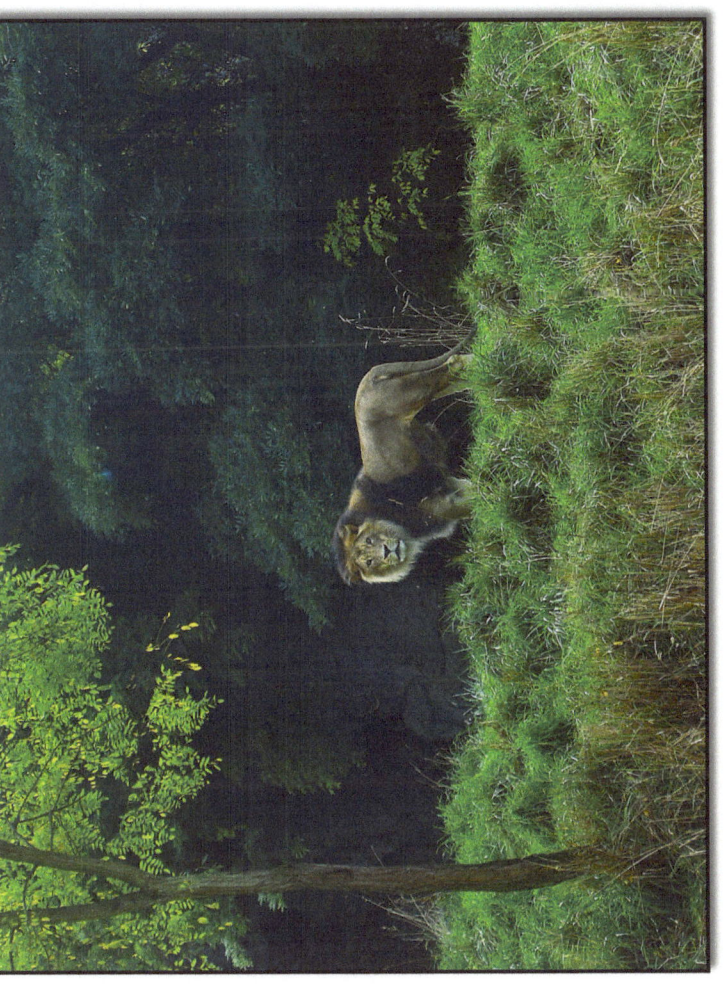

In the jungle, lions live in families called prides.
They hunt together chasing other animals' hides.
Although the female lions makes the kill,
it is the males who first eat their fill.

Then the lionesses have their lunch,
followed by the cubs ~ always a hungry bunch.

## Lion in the Zoo

Far from his African home,
the lion longs for vast areas to roam.

The zoo does its best,
to create a landscape,
that gives him some pleasure
without an escape.

We drive from our homes
to visit him there.
We are impressed with his muscles,
claws and great halo of hair.

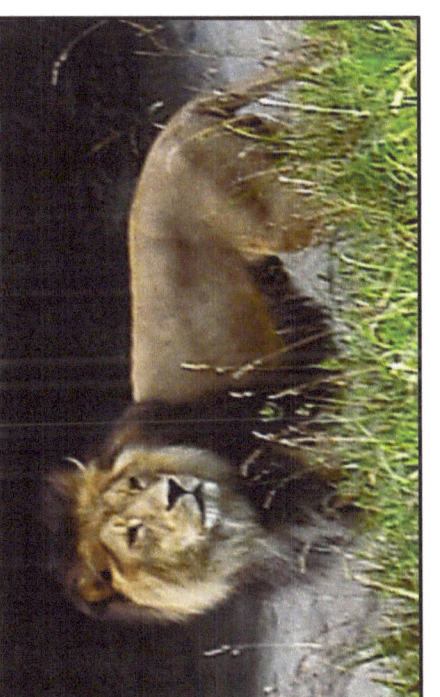

# Elephants

Elephants enjoy family life.
They help each other in times of strife.
In the wild they move about together,
searching for food and a big mud hole.

When the elephants find water,
they splash and they play.
Using their noses for hoses,
they inhale it and spray.

Pachyderms remember everything ~
the good and the bad.
So, don't ever make an elephant mad!

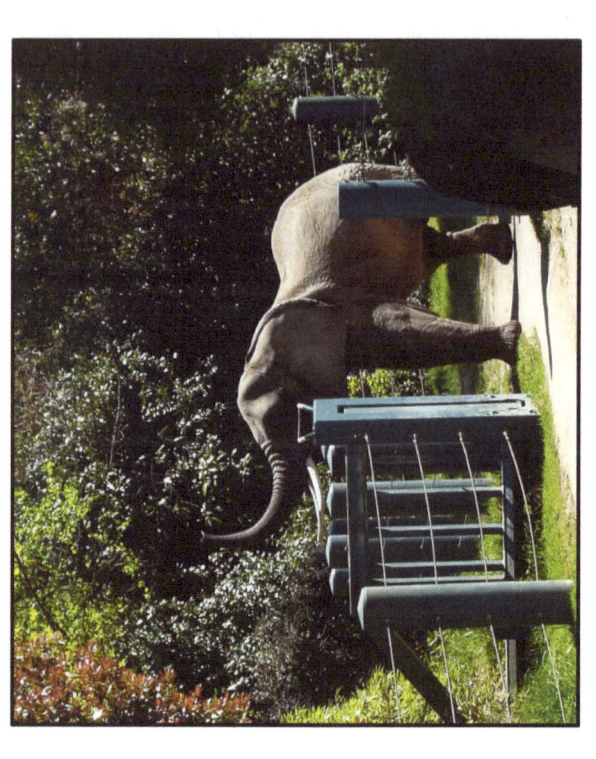

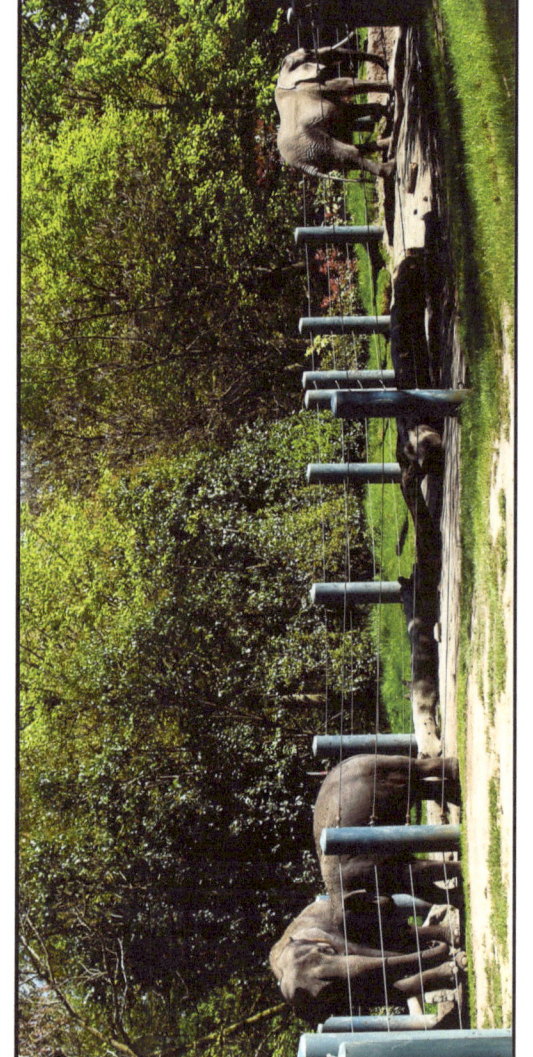

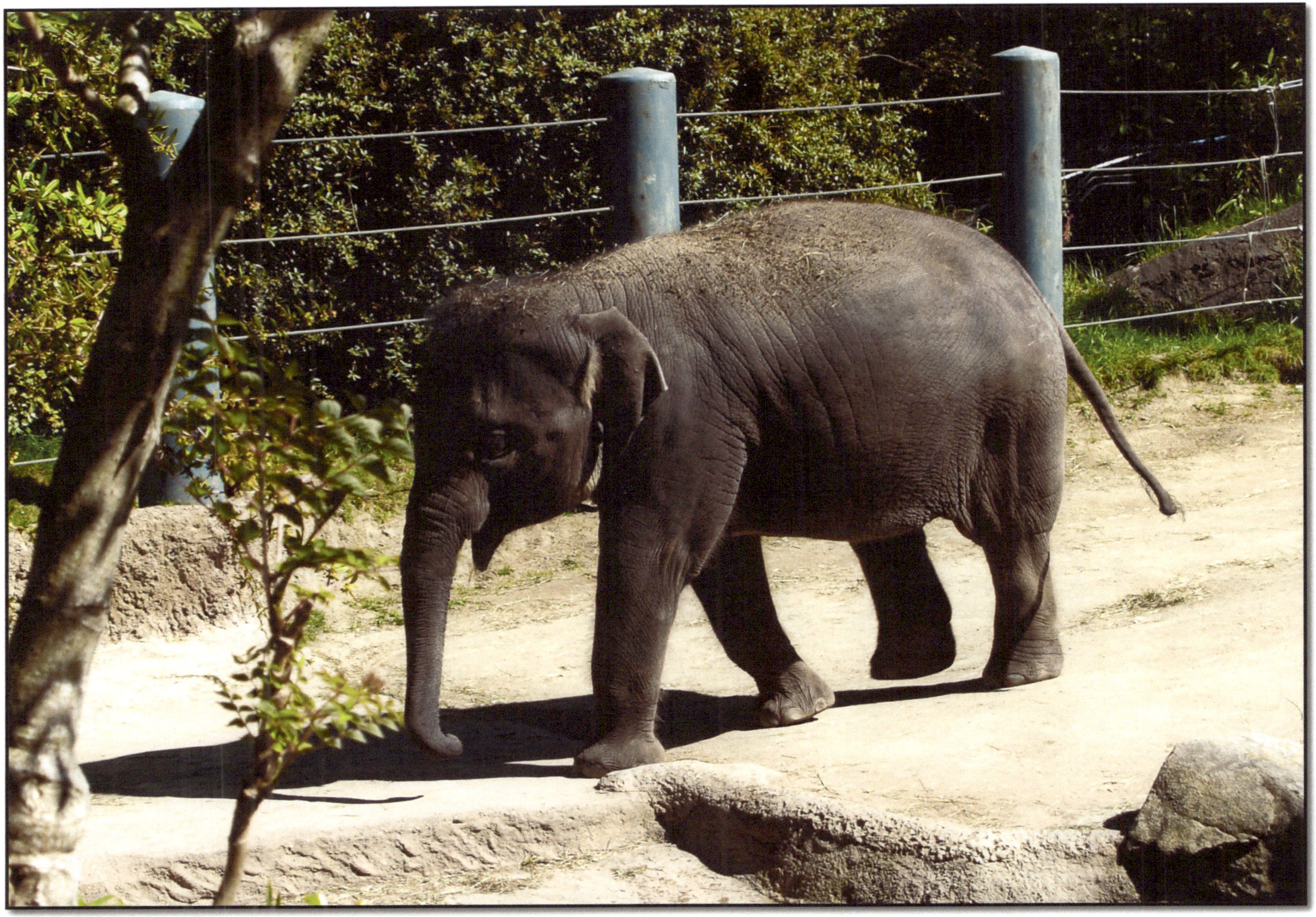

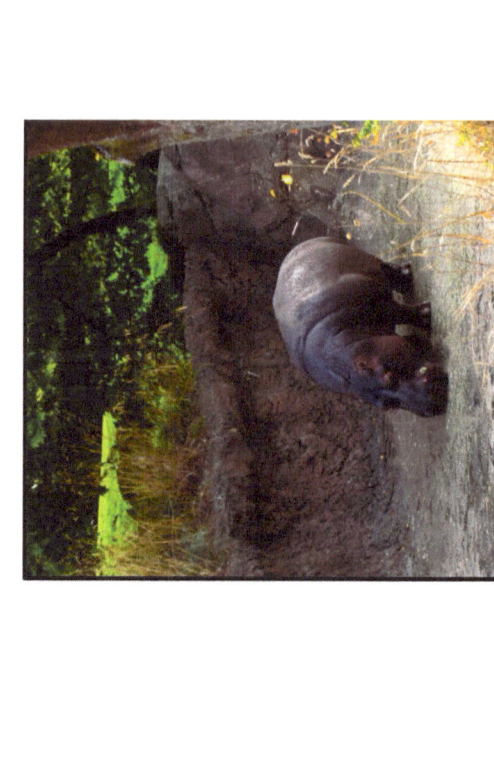

## Hippopotamus

Round and fat,
looking a bit like a pig,
a hippopotamus *is* mighty big.

They like to live near a river or lake.
Hippos can float beneath the water,
holding their breath with barely a break.

Though somewhat scary to see,
it's good to know they are vegetarians,
and don't want to eat you or me.

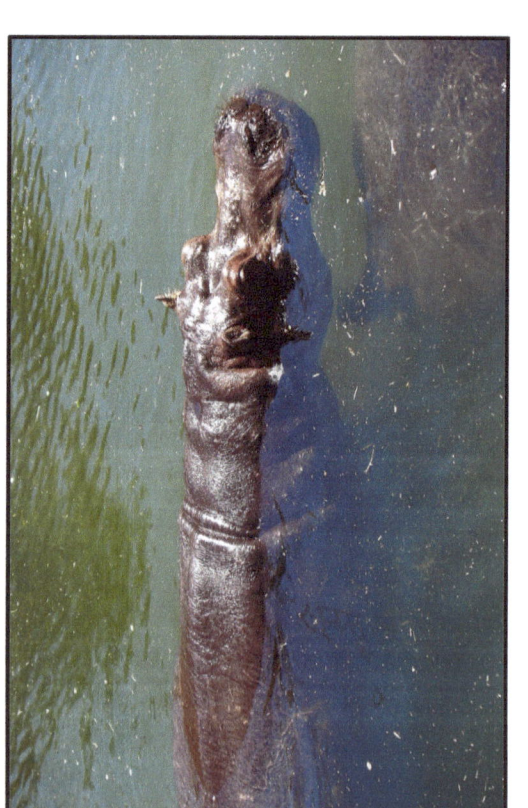

# Zebras

Some people think that zebras
are horses with stripes,
because they look like similar types.

But, no, that's not true.
Zebras are wild and have a bare backside.
You'll never see them with cowboys out for a ride.

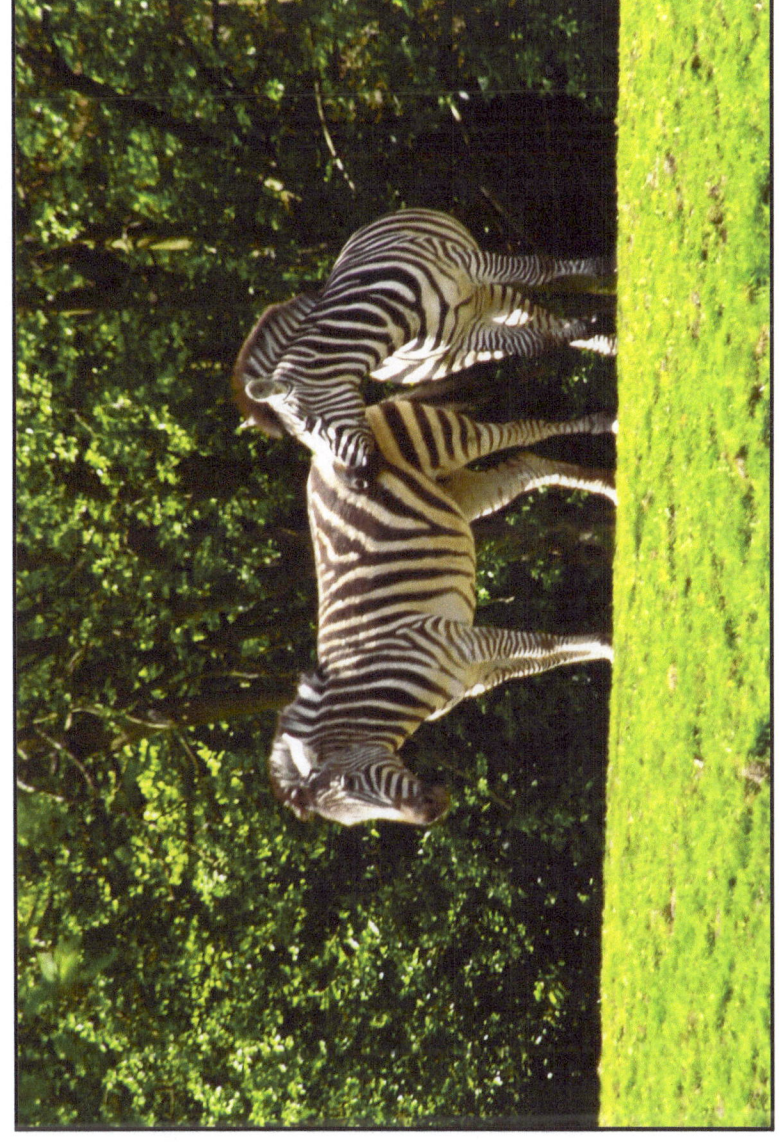

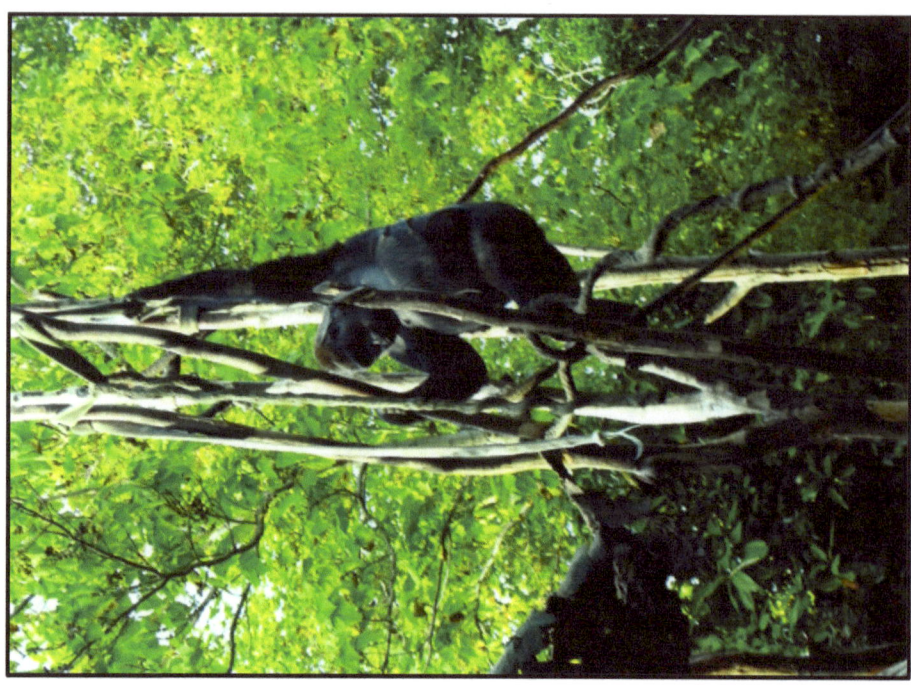

## Gorillas Hanging Out

Watching them swing from tree to tree,
I'd have to say, "Gorillas look a lot like me".

Yet, their bodies are all covered in fur,
and their arms almost reach the ground.

But, when you look in their eyes and see them walk,
you can't help but think, they might even talk.

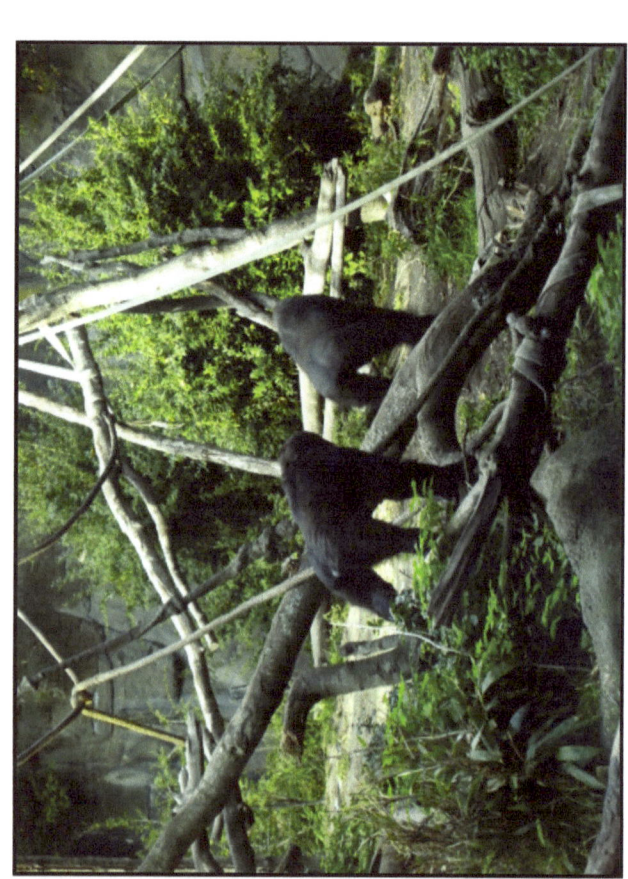

Gorillas eat fruits, leaves and plants.
They also lick sticks covered with ants.

They live in families like people do.
These mammals like to play, climb trees,
and pick bugs off each other.

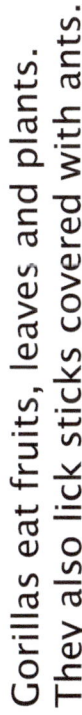

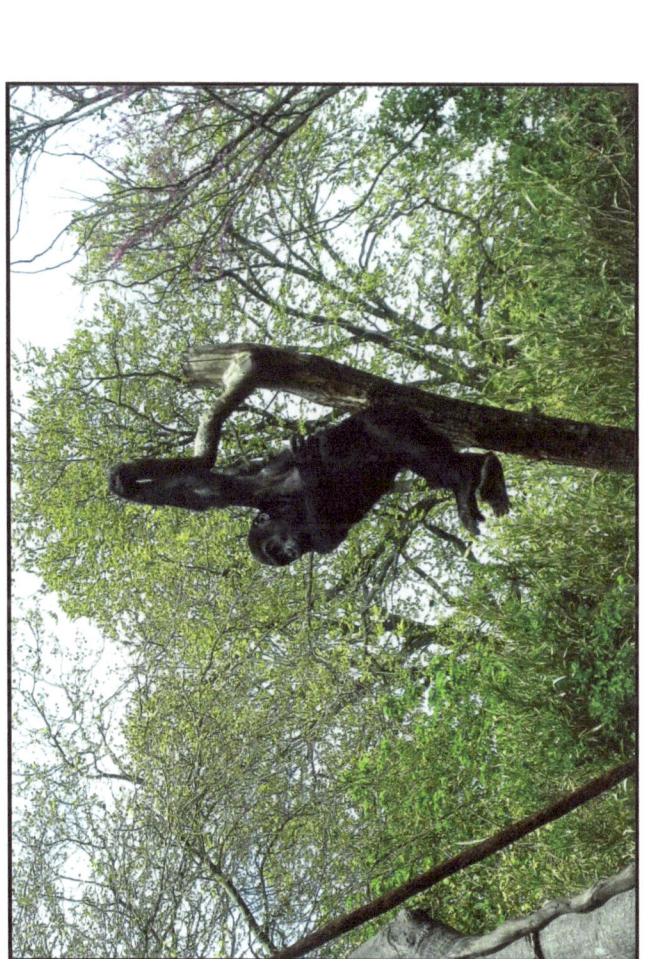

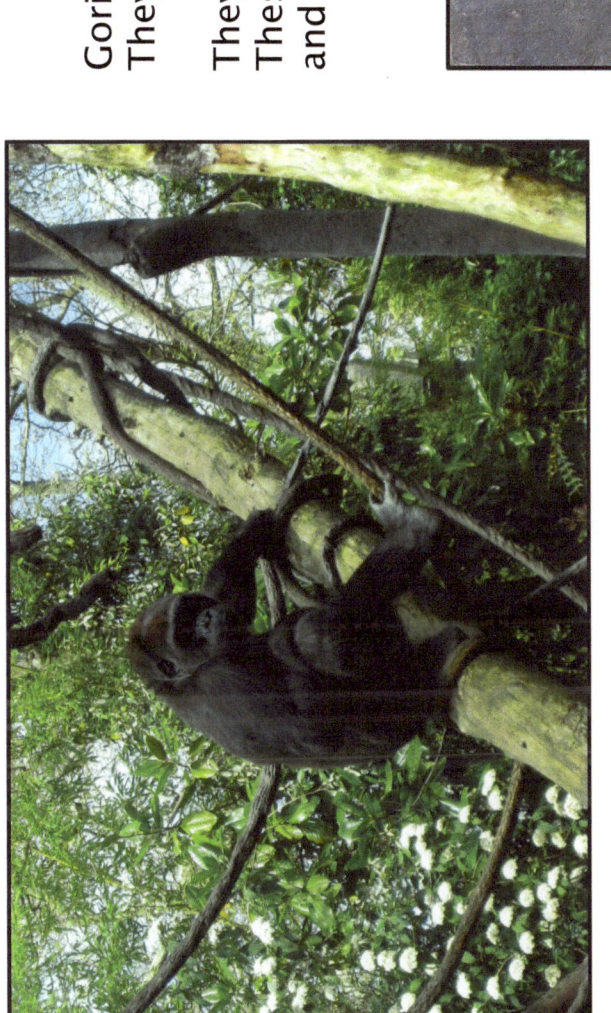

## White Wolf Comes to Me

The white wolf sat atop the hill
looking down at me.
Rescued as pups, she and her brothers
now roam free in their wooded refuge.

Wanting a closer view, I climbed the path.
She followed me with her eyes
as I walked towards her.
From a distance I admired her regal look.

I whistled softly in the wolf's direction,
and was thrilled at my good fortune
when she responded to my call.

White Wolf walked over to me.
Standing together for a long while,
we looked into each others eyes.

She gave me the grace of her presence.
I told her how beautiful she was,
and thanked her for coming to me.

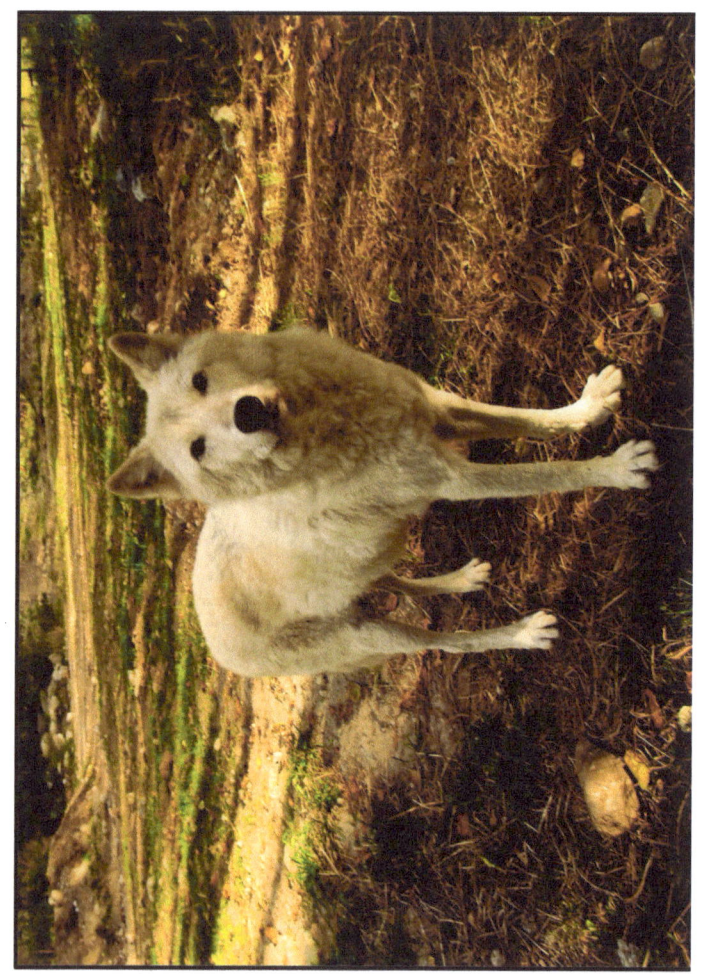

# Bears

Bears as toys, are cuddly enough.
But, in real life,
they are much more
than stuffing and fluff.

They have long, sharp claws,
big teeth and powerful jaws.
Bears eat berries on bushes
and salmon from the streams.

But, you never know
when they might have a fit,
and think that you could be
a tasty little bit.

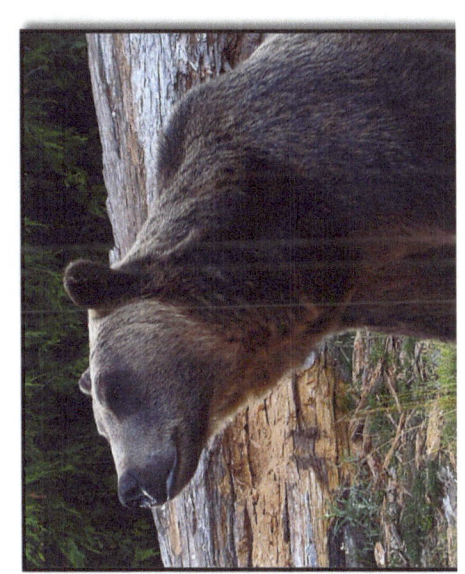

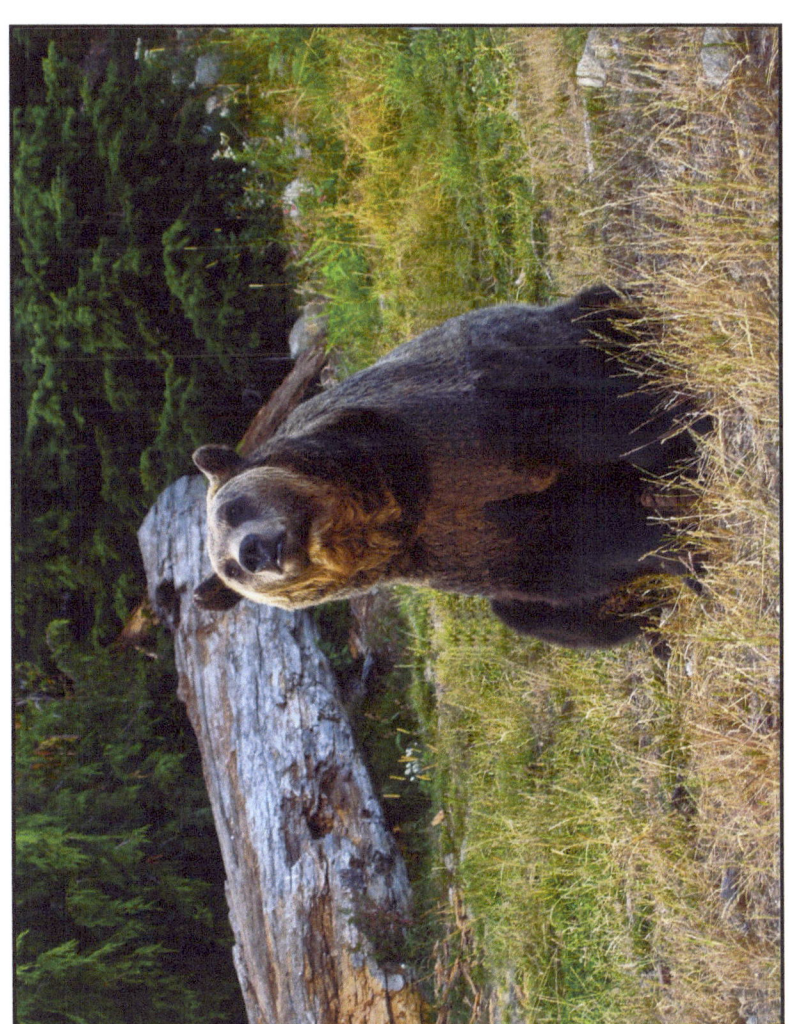

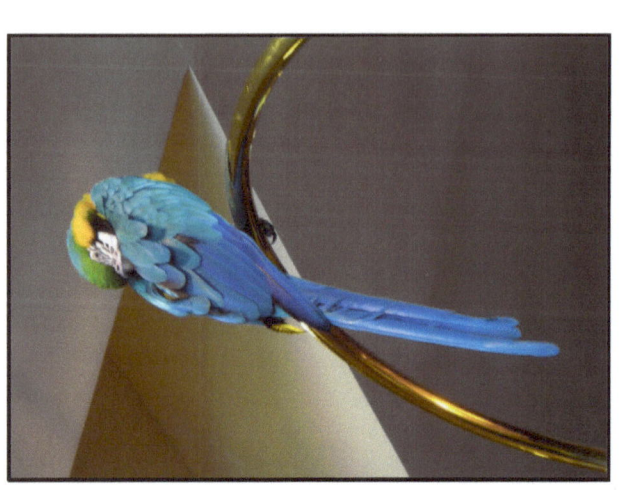

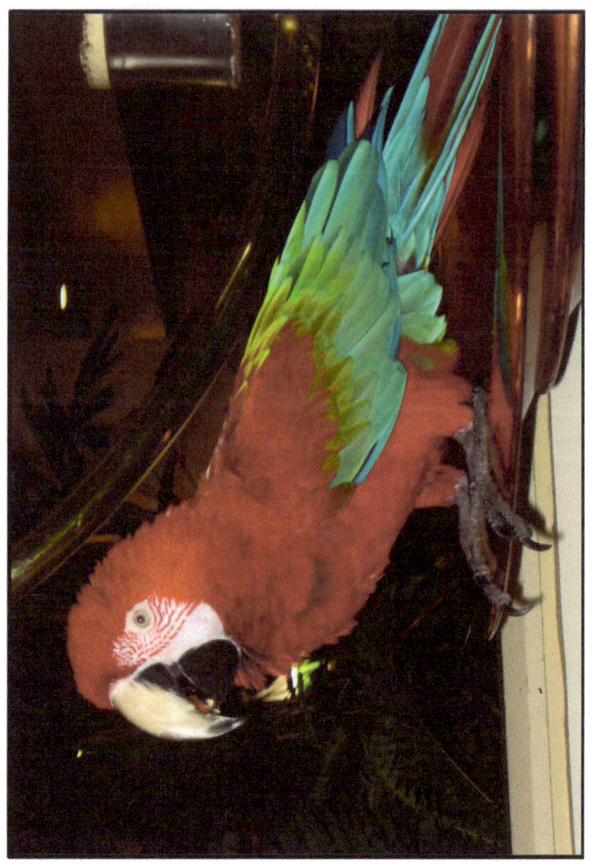

# Parrots ~ Birds That Can Talk

Parrots are large birds that can speak.
Who would have thought that words
could come out of a beak?

Wearing feathers of red, blue and green,
they are a most fantastic sight to be seen!

Bright as the flowers in the jungle
from which they came,
parrots can be wild or they can be tame.

People who live with these birds
insist that parrots understand their words.
~ a nice example of nature with a twist.

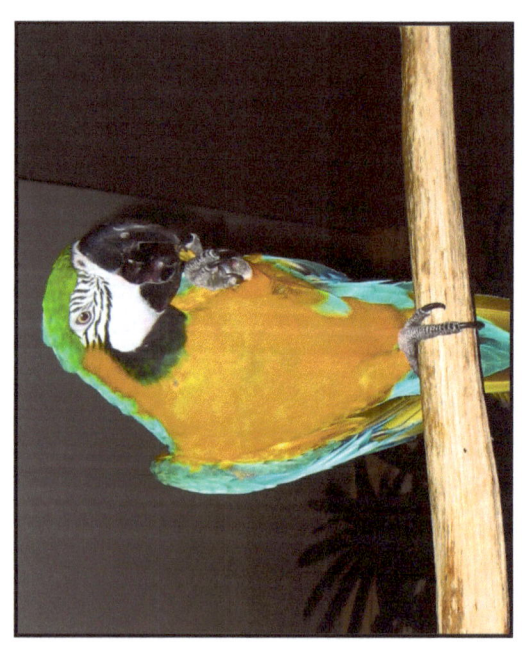

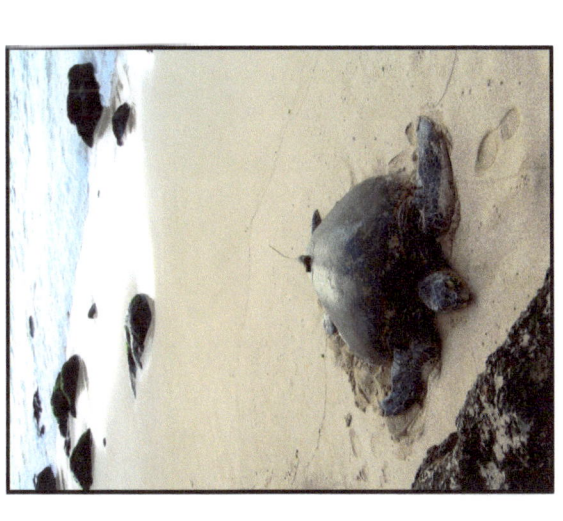

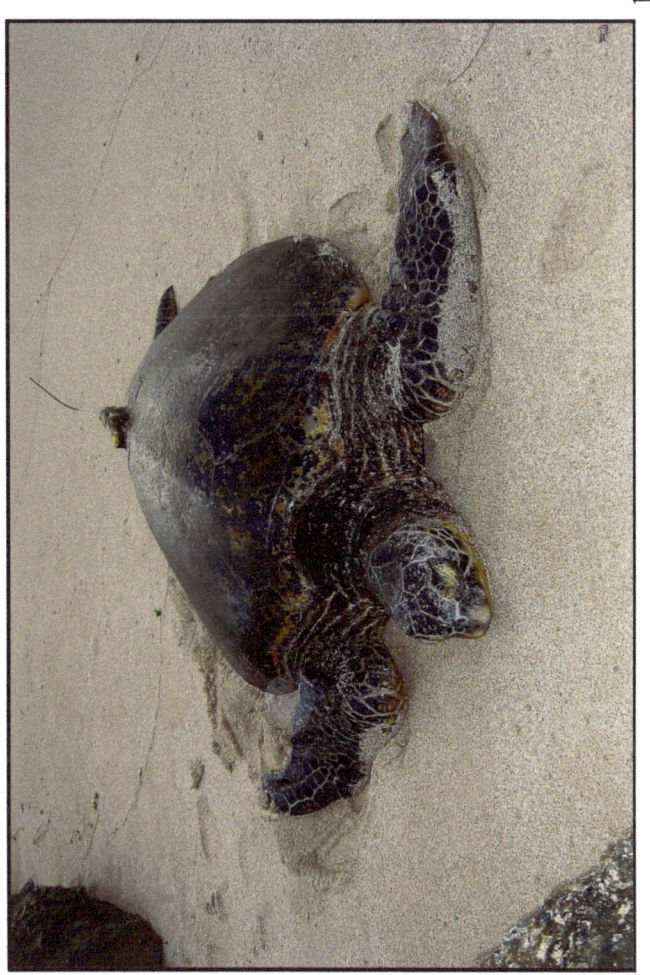

# Giant Sea Turtle

The giant sea turtle
decided to have some fun.
He lumbered out of the water
to bask in the afternoon sun.

He lay like a rock, all still and serene,
unaware that a radio was stuck to his back.
Scientists weren't trying to be mean.
To learn his habits, they used it to track.

Still, I don't like to see it,
but didn't know how to free it.

Sea turtles don't scurry,
and they don't seem to worry.
Maybe that's why
they can live to be 100 years old.

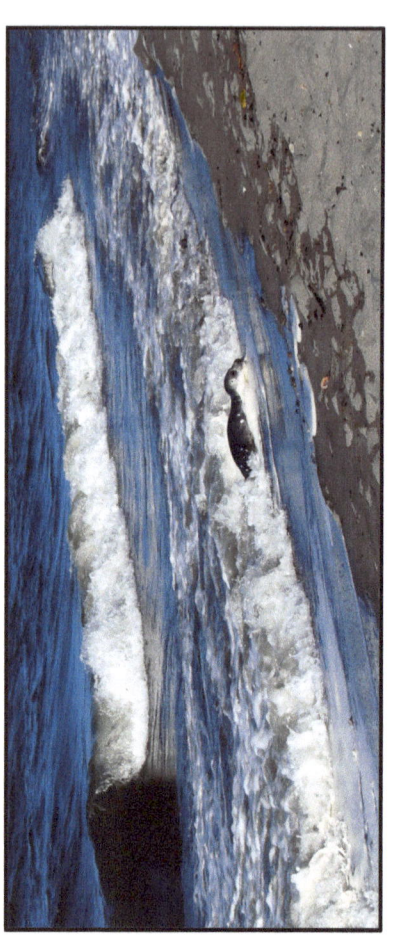

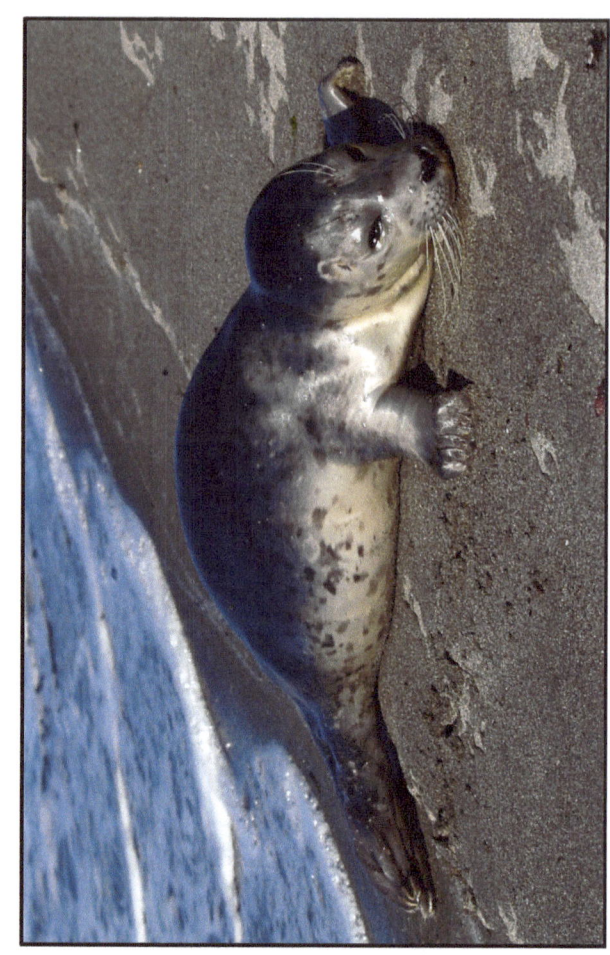

## Meeting a Baby Seal

I was walking down the beach,
when suddenly he was within my reach.
A baby seal, tossing in the surf
was spit out onto the sandy earth.

The creature from the sea lay at my feet.
With big dark eyes, he looked very sweet.
His silky coat I did admire,
but had to resist the desire
to touch him.

When the seal's mother went fishing,
she pushed him towards the land
to wait for her on the gritty sand.
Momma seal would soon be back
with a fish for her baby's snack.

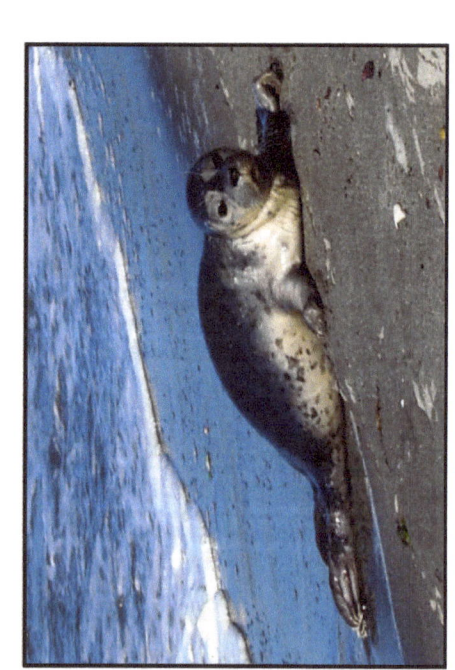

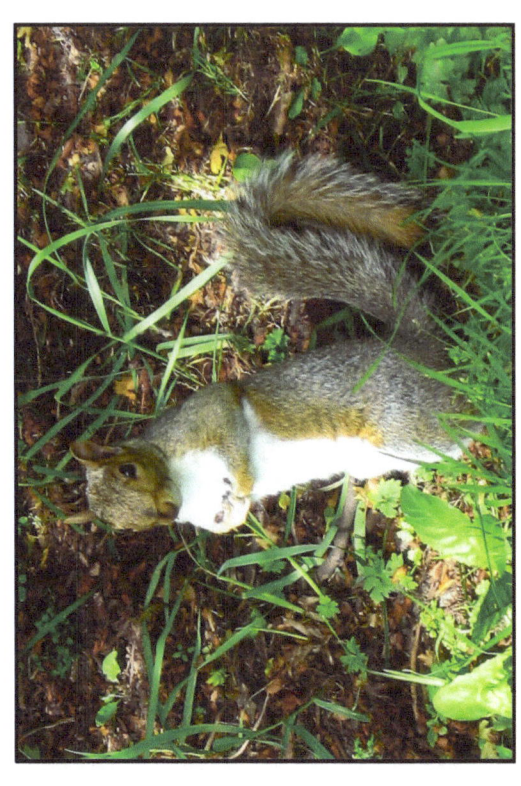

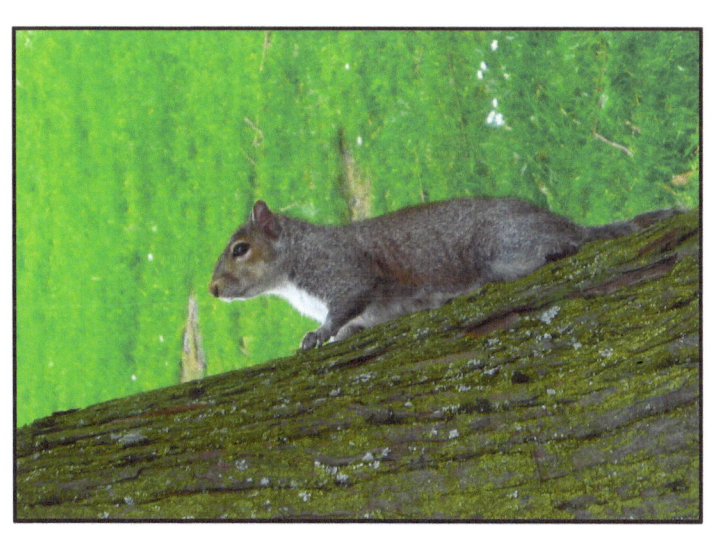

## Squirrels

Our parks are home to lots of squirrels.
They run about, waving that big tail that curls.
Dogs will chase them until they run up a tree.
Those rodents are really fast as can be.

Squirrels like nuts and bury them for winter food.
There are no squirrel stores where they can shop.
They eat what they've hidden,
and then they won't drop.

Squirrels look cute, yet have a dangerous bite.
So when you seem them, leave them alone,
and just enjoy the squirrely sight.

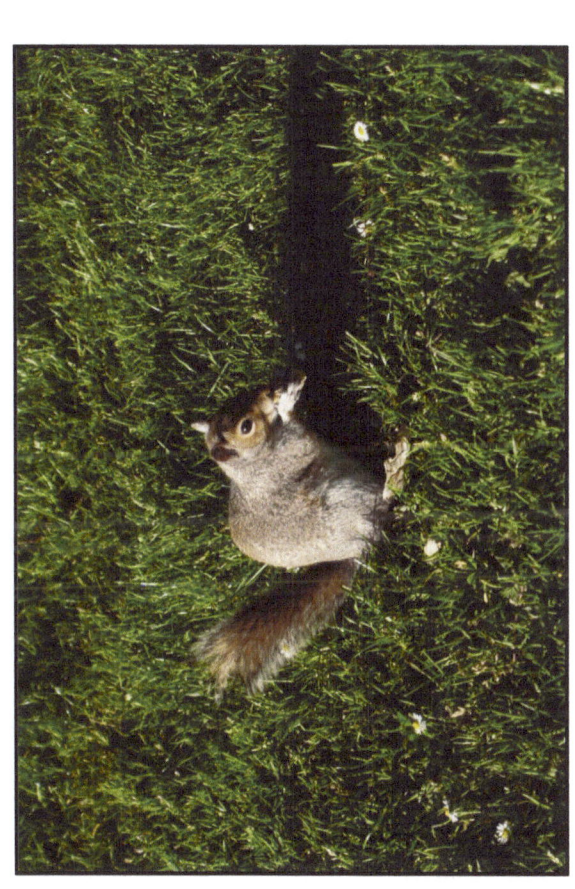

## Mama Duck with Her Ducklings

Ducklings follow their mother
wherever she goes.

Swimming in the water or walking on land,
mama duck leads her furry babies
to food and safety.

She cares for them
until they are ready to fly away.
Our mothers do that too.

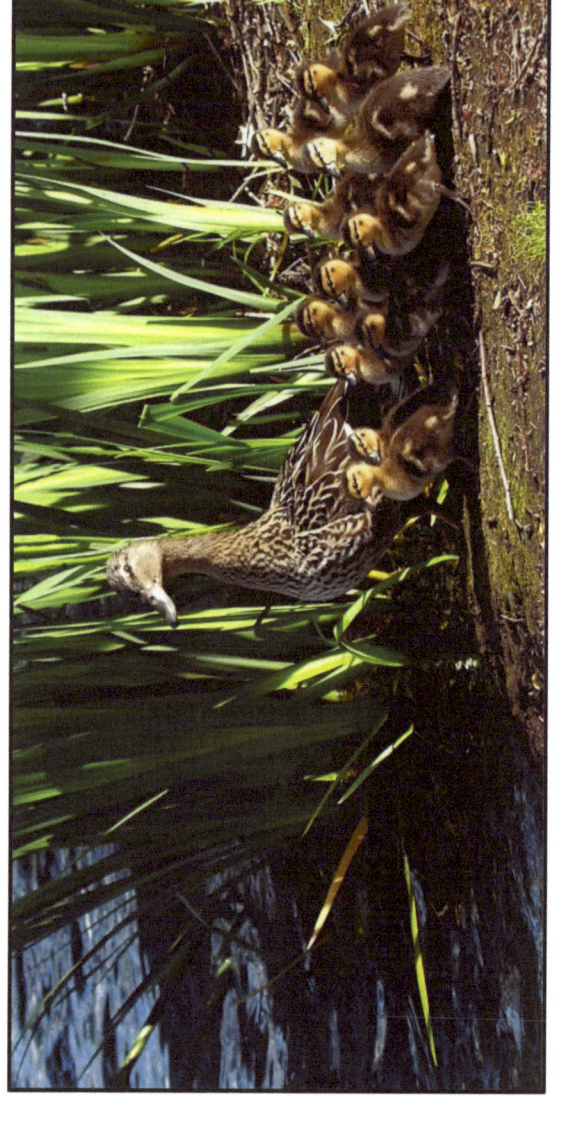

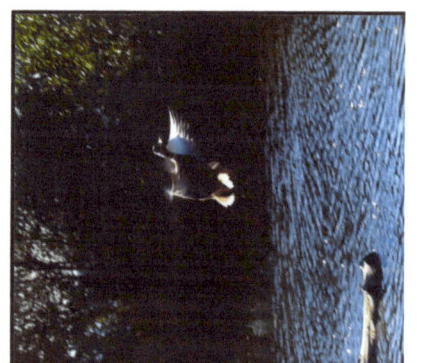

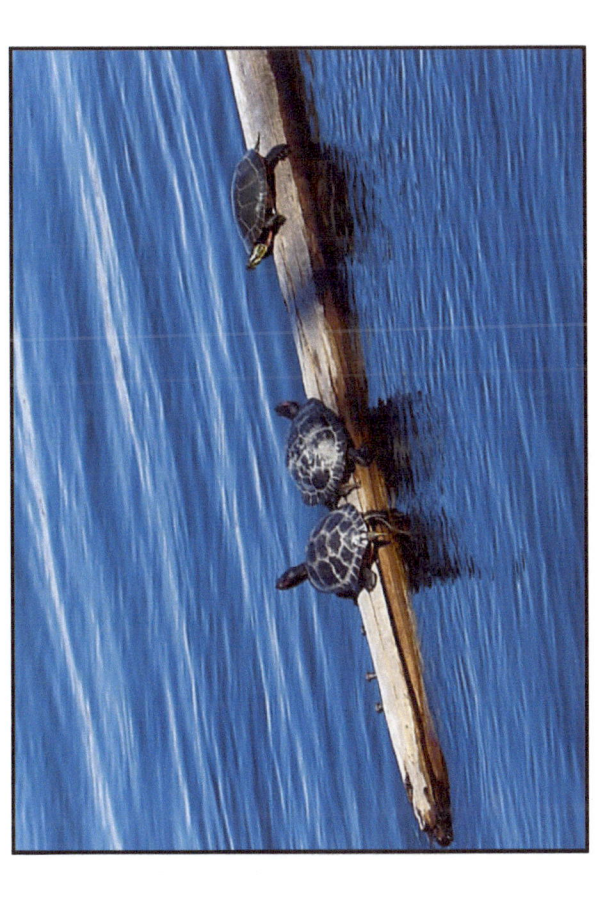

## Turtles at the Lake

Lined up on a log, by the shore of a lake,
turtles lay relaxing in the sun.

Their shells look like upside down plates,
where sometimes their heads will hide.

They don't move much,
and as such, are hard to know.

I haven't heard them make any noise,
nor, have I seen them play with toys.

But, turtles floating on a log
sure make the lake look nice.

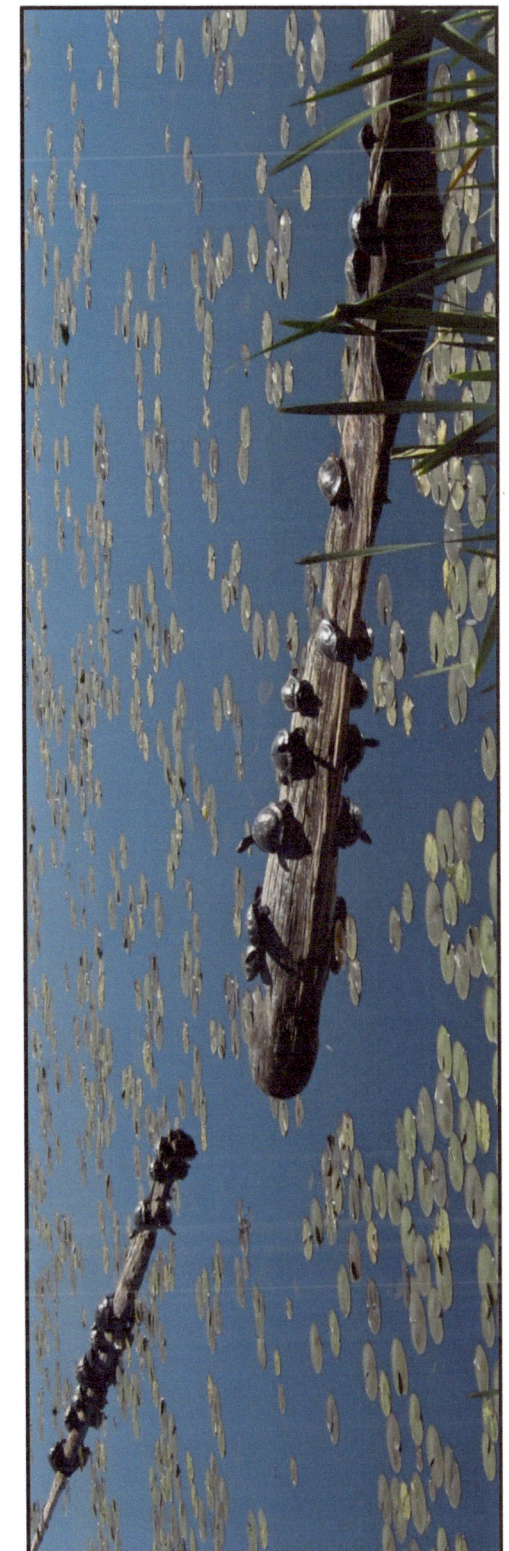

# Dogs

Little Bindi and big Max so mild,
our pets became dogs gone wild.

They were put in the yard to play,
but the naughty dogs, they ran away.

We thought they would just hang;
instead, they started running with a bang.

First Max, then Bindi ...
they left us quick as can be

We chased them and gave call,
but they didn't hear us at all.

Something inside the dogs made them go.
It's their wolf part that we can never know.

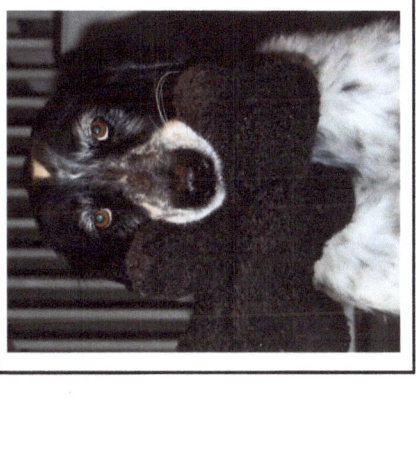

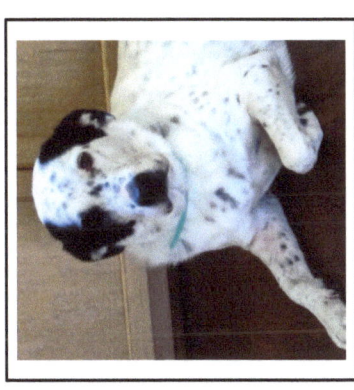

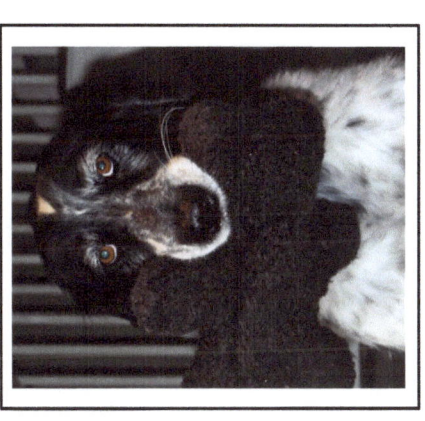

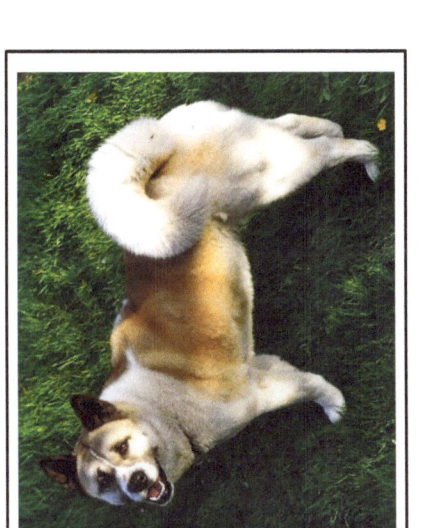

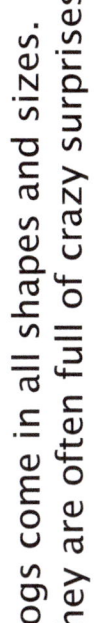

Dogs come in all shapes and sizes.
They are often full of crazy surprises.

Your food, their food, they'll quickly eat.
Dogs will do tricks to earn a good treat.

They are known as man's best friend,
because they are loyal to the very end.

If you've ever played with one,
then you know, they are lots of fun!

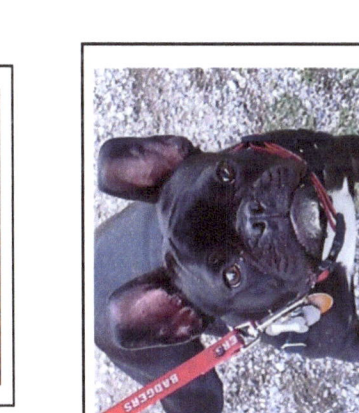

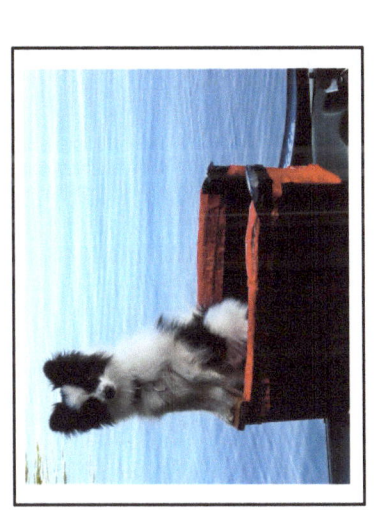

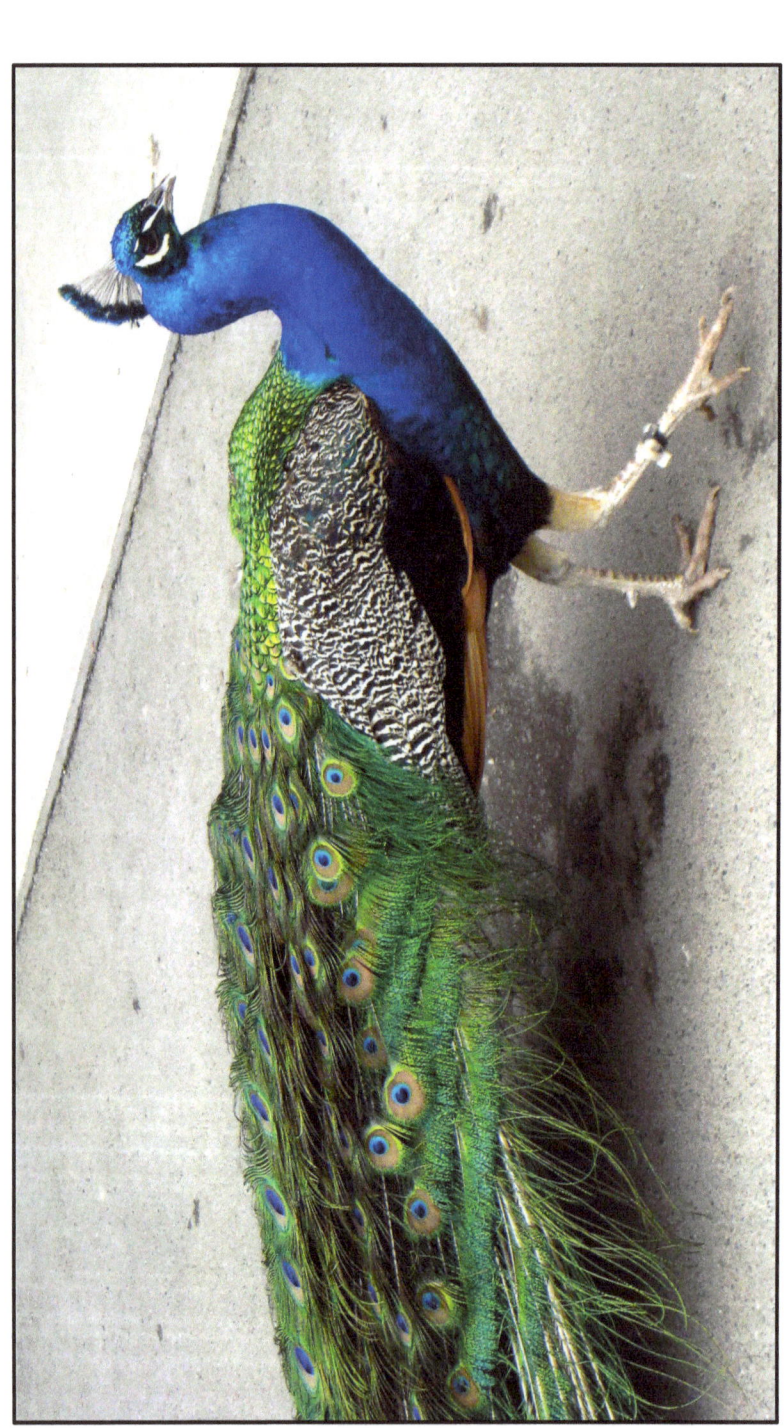

## Peacock

The peacock walks across the pavement,
dragging along its folded arraignment,

If you are lucky, he will shiver and shake,
slowly unfolding his long tail to make
something quite glorious.

An arc forms as the feathers unfold,
like a built–in fan that only he can hold.

Swirls of color, blue and green
create a vision that begs to be seen.

Standing there, proud as can be
he holds his fan up for the world to see.

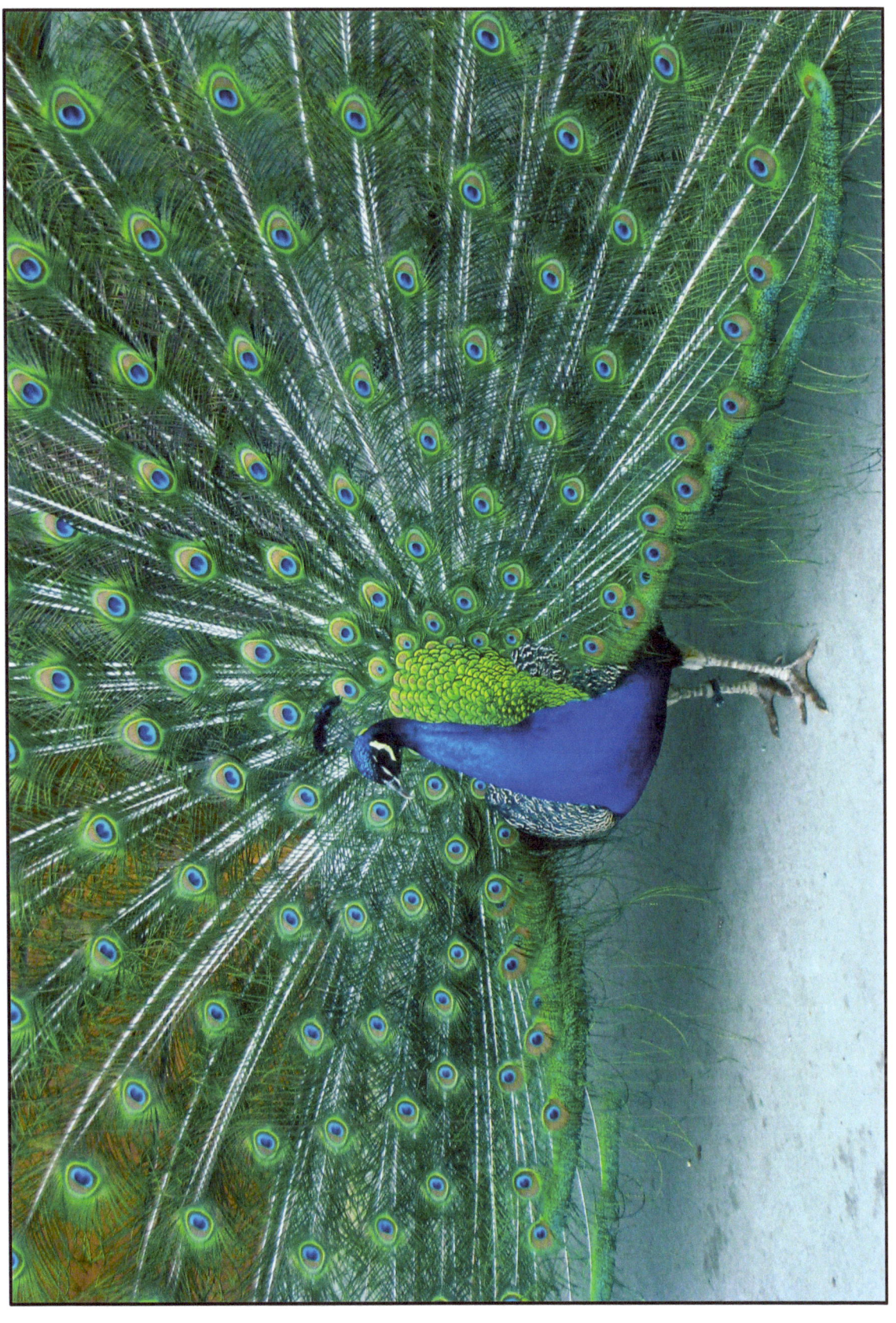

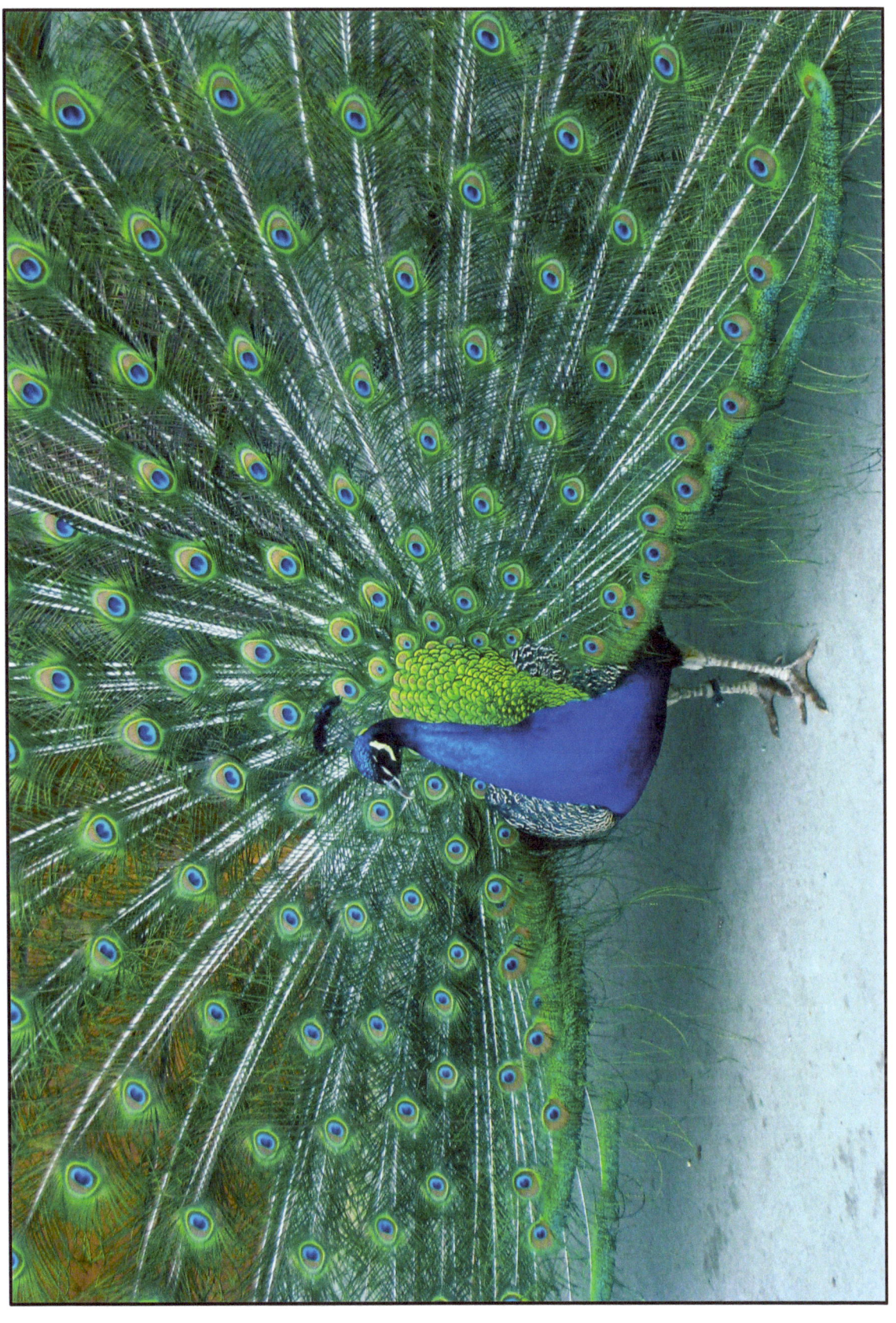

# Who are the animals in your world?

They could be neighbor pets, or creatures that you see at your park, zoo or wild places. Put their names, or the kind of animal they are on the lines. Then you can draw pictures or put photos in the empty boxes.

www.ingramcontent.com/pod-product-compliance
Lightning Source LLC
Chambersburg PA
CBHW040754200526
45159CB00025B/2466